Get Started With
STEM

What's the Season?

by Ruth Owen

Ruby Tuesday Books

Published in 2017 by Ruby Tuesday Books Ltd.

Copyright © 2017 Ruby Tuesday Books Ltd.

Editor: Mark J. Sachner
Designer: Emma Randall
Consultant: Judy Wearing, PhD, BEd
Production: John Lingham

Photo credits
Alamy: 12, 18 (top), 21 (top), 27, 28 (top), 31 (top); FLPA: 15 (top), 15 (bottom), 26; Istock Photo: 13 (top), 15 (center); Public Domain: 25 (top); Shutterstock: Cover, 1, 2, 4–5, 6–7, 8–9, 10–11, 13 (bottom), 14, 16–17, 18 (bottom), 19, 20, 21 (center), 21 (bottom), 22–23, 24, 25 (bottom), 28 (bottom), 29, 30, 31 (bottom).

Library of Congress Control Number: 2016918447

ISBN 978-1-911341-45-1

Printed and published in the United States of America

For further information including rights and permissions requests, please contact our Customer Service Department at 877-337-8577.

Contents

Words shown in **bold** in the text are explained in the glossary.

The download button shows there are free worksheets or other resources available. Go to:

www.rubytuesdaybooks.com/getstarted

What's the Season?

Every year there are four seasons—spring, summer, autumn, and winter.

As the seasons change, the days get longer or shorter.

The weather changes, too.

Each season lasts for about three months.

The Seasons

Winter — December, January, February

Spring — March, April, May

Summer — June, July, August

Autumn — September, October, November

A

B

C

D

E

Check It Out!

Look at the pictures on these pages.

What season is it in each of the pictures?

(The answers are below.)

Answers: E and F are spring; B and H are summer; A and C are autumn; D and G are winter.

F

G

H

Day and Night

As the seasons change, the length of day and night changes, too.

In spring, days gradually become longer.

A day is 24 hours long. Daytime begins when the Sun rises and ends when it sets. When the Sun is not in the sky, it is dark and nighttime.

By summer there are more hours of daytime than nighttime.

It might still be light when you go to bed!

As summer changes to autumn, days gradually become shorter.

Summer 4:00 pm

By winter, there are more hours of nighttime than daytime.

It might even be dark as you travel home from school!

Winter 4:00 pm

Let's Test It!

Are the days getting longer or shorter?

1. During spring or autumn, choose a day of the week.

2. Each week on that day, draw one clock that shows the time of sunrise and one that shows the time of sunset.

   How much longer or shorter is daytime after one week?

   How about after four weeks?

   Is daytime getting longer or shorter?

March 1

Sunrise
7:00 am

Sunset
5:30 pm

(If you don't know what time the Sun rose, ask an adult to help you find out online.)

Spring Is Here!

Once spring arrives, the days get longer and the weather warms up. Sometimes it can still be very cold at night, though.

Check It Out!

Look at these pictures.

Which of the outfits do you think would be best to wear on a spring day where you live? Why?

Be a Scientist!

Thermometer

We use a thermometer to measure temperature.

The liquid inside goes up or down as the temperature rises or falls.

The top of the liquid shows the temperature.

The temperature is 50°F (10°C).

To measure temperature, we use units of measurement called degrees Fahrenheit or degrees Celsius. We can write "degrees Fahrenheit" as °F and "degrees Celsius" as °C.

What's the temperature in spring where you live?

During four weeks in spring, record the temperature once a week.

1. Place a thermometer outdoors.

2. Each week on the same day and at the same time, record the temperature on the thermometer.

3. You can show your results on a graph like the one below.

Did the temperature go up or down or stay the same over the four weeks?

What do you think the temperature might be in weeks 5 and 6? Write down your ideas and then check how close you get.

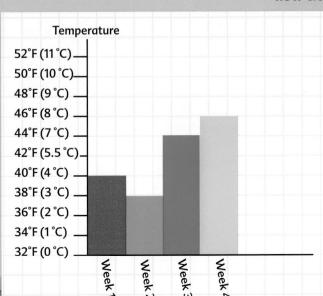

Time to Get Growing

When warm spring weather arrives, plants start growing.

Under the ground, daffodil **bulbs** have been waiting for spring.

Daffodil shoots

New **shoots** sprout from the bulbs and grow into leaves and flowers.

In winter, grass plants stop growing. When spring arrives, new blades of grass burst from the ground.

Grass in winter

Grass in spring

Fat, green buds sprout from bare tree branches.

Bud

Leaves

The buds unfold and become leaves or flowers called blossoms.

Blossoms

Apple trees in spring

Time to Build Nests

It's spring, and birds are building nests where they will lay eggs and care for their chicks.

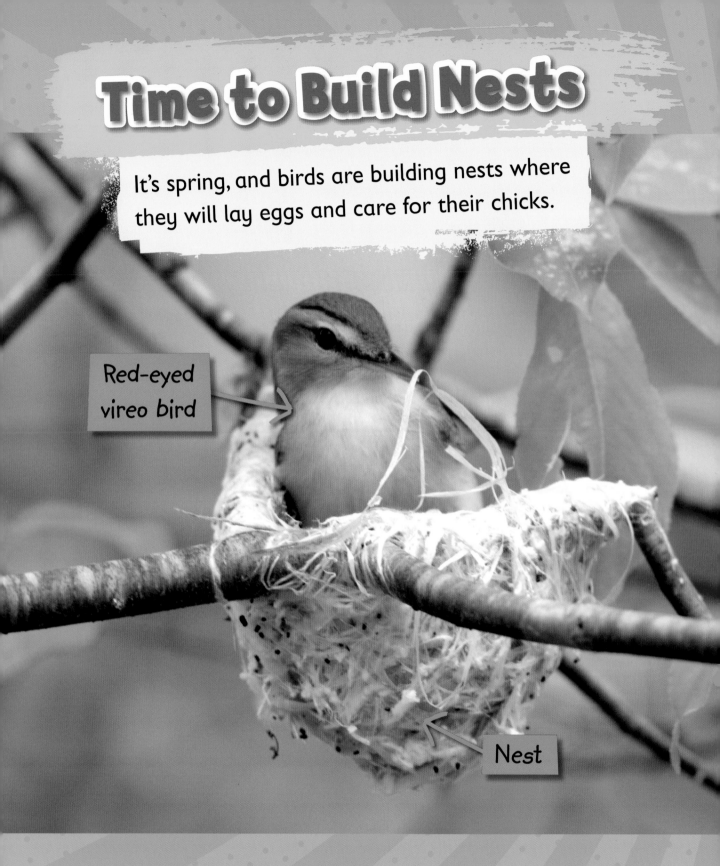

Red-eyed vireo bird

Nest

A red-eyed vireo builds a nest from bark, grass, and other plant material.

The nest measures just 2 inches (5 cm) across!

Female robin

Nest

Eggs

A female robin lays up to five blue eggs in her nest.

Swallows build a nest of mud and grass in a barn, garage, or other building.

They use their beaks to collect mud from puddles and ponds.

Adult swallow feeding a chick

Nest

Spring Babies

Many animals have their babies in spring. At this time of year, there's lots of food around.

Sheep give birth to their lambs. The lambs drink milk from their mothers and eat new, green grass.

 Let's Explore!

Go on a spring treasure hunt in a garden, yard, park, or forest.

Try to spot as many things on this list as possible. Don't touch or disturb the animals you see.

- *A new green shoot on the ground*
- *A bud on a tree branch*
- *A caterpillar*

- *A bird with nesting material in its beak*
- *A colorful flower*
- *A baby animal*
- *Sunlight coming through trees*
- *Something with a nice smell*
- *Blossoms*
- *A ladybug*

Caterpillars

Many types of butterflies lay their eggs in spring. Caterpillars hatch from the eggs and hungrily feed on leaves.

Butterfly

Father robin

Robins hunt for worms and caterpillars to feed to their chicks.

A mother fox catches a baby bird to feed to her cubs.

15

Summer Is Here!

As spring changes to summer, the weather gets much warmer. It may even be hot at night.

Colorful flowers grow in gardens and parks.

Bees, butterflies, and other insects visit flowers to drink a sweet juice called nectar.

Check It Out!

This thermometer shows the temperature on a hot summer day.

What is the temperature?

(The answer is below.)

Answer: The temperature on the thermometer is 90°F (32°C).

Apples grow fat and juicy on the branches of apple trees.

Grass can grow so fast during summer that people need to mow it.

Sometimes in summer there is heavy rain. There may even be storms with flashing lightning and crashing thunder.

A Summer Feast

All summer, animals are busy finding food and eating.

Aphid

Ladybug

Ladybugs feed on aphids and other tiny insects.

Let's Explore!

Go on a summer treasure hunt in a garden, yard, park, or forest.

Try to spot as many things on this list as possible. Don't touch or disturb the animals you see.

- *A bee visiting flowers*
- *A butterfly*
- *Moss*
- *Something red*
- *A place where a small animal could hide*
- *A baby bird begging its parent for food*
- *Some long grass*
- *A spiderweb*
- *Tree roots*
- *A flower with more than six petals*
- *A feather*
- *Something symmetrical*

• A leaf that's been chewed

At night, snails slither from plant to plant munching on leaves.

If the weather gets too hot, a snail takes shelter inside its shell. It may stay like this for several months, until the weather cools down.

Sparrow chick

Father sparrow

Baby birds are ready to leave their nests.

They beg their parents for food.

Autumn Is Here!

As summer comes to an end, the weather gets cooler and autumn arrives.

This season can be a time for heavy rain, strong winds, and storms.

Frost

Sometimes at night it gets so cold that icy **frost** forms on grass, leaves, and everything outside.

In autumn, many plants produce seeds and then die.

The leaves on some trees turn yellow, red, orange, and brown and drop to the ground.

Apple tree

Acorn

Let's Talk

What do you think happens to the leaves that fall from trees in autumn?

Acorns, horse chestnut seeds, and apples also fall from trees.

Horse chestnut seed

21

Eating, Recycling, and Storing

When autumn leaves fall to the ground, worms help recycle them into new soil. How?

Worm

Worms eat dead, rotting leaves and soil.

Inside their bodies, this mixture becomes leafy, muddy poop that gets mixed into the soil.

Wood mouse

When winter comes, there might not be much to eat.

So in autumn, some animals store food to last through winter.

Blackberry

Many kinds of mice gather berries, acorns, and seeds. They store this food in their nests or homes, called burrows.

Squirrels gather acorns and bury them in the ground.

Fantastic Fungi

If you visit a park or woodland in autumn, you might spot **fungi**, such as toadstools.

Toadstool

BE CAREFUL!
Many fungi are poisonous. Never touch fungi you see growing in a woodland, field, or any other outdoor place.

Fungus

Many types of fungi feed on fallen leaves and dead trees.

They get the **nutrients** they need to live from dead plant material.

Scarlet elfcup fungus

Without fungi, layer upon layer of plant material would pile up on the ground in a woodland.

As they feed, fungi make wood and dead leaves rot and become crumbly.

Then this plant material becomes part of the soil.

 Let's Explore!

Go on an autumn treasure hunt in a garden, yard, park, or forest.

Try to spot as many things on this list as possible. Don't touch or disturb the animals you see.

- *A dead flower with seeds*
- *Red berries on a tree or bush*
- *An acorn*
- *A horse chestnut seed in a spiky case*
- *A pine cone*
- *A worm under dead leaves*

- *Fungi*
- *An animal footprint in mud*
- *A bird bathing in a puddle*
- *Rotting wood*
- *An empty bird's nest*
- *A leaf with two or more autumn colors*

Ready for Winter

Swallows spend the summer zooming through the skies catching flies. As summer ends, though, there are fewer flies to eat.

Swallow

In autumn, swallows **migrate**, or make a long flight, to South America, where there are plenty of insects to eat.

Fly

When spring comes they fly back to North America.

Swallows often gather on telephone wires before setting off on their long migration.

When the weather gets cold, a groundhog goes into its cozy, underground burrow.

It falls into a deep sleep called **hibernation** until spring.

Let's Talk

A groundhog doesn't eat all winter.
How do you think it stays alive without food?
(The answer is at the bottom of the page.)

Answer: A groundhog eats as much as possible in the summer. By autumn, it has a lot of body fat. During its long winter hibernation, the groundhog lives off its fat.

Winter Is Here!

Winter is the coldest season of the year. The weather is often windy and stormy.

In some areas, snow may fall.

In winter, the temperature may drop to 32°F (0°C). When this happens, the water in puddles and ponds freezes.

Freezing point

In winter, it's too cold for many trees and other plants to grow.

The plants look as if they have died, but they are just resting.

When spring comes, they will grow new leaves.

 Let's Explore!

Go on a winter treasure hunt in a garden, yard, park, or forest.

Try to spot as many things on this list as possible. Don't touch or disturb the animals you see.

- *Animal footprint in snow or mud*
- *A tree with bare branches*
- *Berries on a branch*
- *A dead flower*
- *Your breath in the cold air*
- *A bird looking for food*

- *An evergreen tree*
- *Melting ice*
- *A hole in a tree*
- *A brown leaf*
- *A rotting log*
- *Frozen water*
- *New green shoots*
- *A holly leaf*

The Toughest Season

In winter, birds and other wild animals may struggle to find food.

People help birds by filling bird feeders with nuts and seeds.

Northern cardinal

Food can be scarce in winter because plants stop producing fruit and seeds. Also, the insects that birds and other animals eat die or hide away.

Squirrels dig up the acorns they buried in autumn.

Sometimes they visit bird feeders for a filling meal!

Let's Talk

What's the season right now? How can you tell? Which season do you like best? Why?

As winter comes to an end, new green shoots appear. Spring is nearly here....

31

Glossary

bulb (BUHLB)
The rounded underground part that some plants grow from. Food for the new plant is stored in the bulb.

frost (FRAWST)
A thin layer of ice that forms on the ground and other surfaces when the temperature falls below freezing.

fungi (FUHN-jye)
A group of living things that includes mushrooms, toadstools, and mold.

hibernation (hye-bur-NAY-shuhn)
Spending the winter in a deep sleep without eating or drinking.

migrate (MYE-grate)
To move from one place to another as the seasons change. Animals might migrate to find food or to avoid weather that's too hot or too cold.

nutrient (NOO-tree-uhnt)
A substance that a living thing needs to grow and be healthy.

shoot (SHOOT)
A new part of a plant. Shoots grow from seeds and from existing plants.

Index